Colors of Sports

by Laura Purdie Salas

CAPSTONE PRESS

a capstone imprint

The game is in full swing! But maybe you have questions. Which team is she on? Why did the game stop? Did he cross the goal line? Colors answer all of these questions. Let's take a look at the colorful world of sports!

Which football players are on the same team? If all the players wore different pants and shirts, it would be hard to tell. But these **purple** jerseys make it clear. Players can find their teammates in a flash, and fans know who to cheer for.

Soccer players and other athletes play on **green** grass fields. Grass is like a little cushion to run on. Indoor sports fields are green even though the grass is not real.

In hockey, all eyes are on the puck! The **black** rubber disc is easy to see against white ice. Each team tries to shoot the puck into the other team's goal.

Use your trusty **brown** baseball glove to catch a fly ball. Each white Major League baseball has exactly 108 bright **red** stitches.

Do you think all bowling balls are black? No way! They come in neon colors like blaze **orange** and lime **green**. Or do you like **gold** or **blue** better? All these bowling balls shimmer and spin down the alley. Strike!

Olympic **gold** might be the most beautiful color in the world. Every athlete in the Olympic Games wants to win one of these medals. Winning one means you are the best in the world at your sport.

Football referees wear **black** and **white** stripes. This pattern stands out from the players' uniforms. Fans can easily find the referees to see what calls they make.

Bright **orange** basketballs are easy to see. What can you do with a basketball? You can dribble it down the court. You can pass it to another player. And, of course, you can shoot it! Two points!

Figure skaters fly across the ice in glittery costumes. This **pink** outfit shines as the skater spins and leaps. She is a blur of color and speed!

Gymnasts bend and twist. They tumble and roll, leap and land. The gym floor is hard, but **blue** mats cushion it. Gymnasts can make a safe, soft landing.

This boxer's **red** gloves are thick and padded. If he hits without them, he could break the bones in his hand. The gloves also help protect his face.

Uh-oh! Sometimes a football player breaks a rule. Then a referee throws down a bright *yellow* penalty flag. The punishment for breaking the rule is called a penalty. A penalty might mean losing yards, and that can mean losing a football game.

Swimmers wear tight, stretchy swimsuits. Loose suits would drag in the water and slow down a swimmer. Check out this **purple** suit and swim cap!

Glossary

alley—a long, narrow lane down which you roll bowling balls

court—an area where games such as basketball, tennis, and racquetball are played

cushion—to soften the effect of something

dribble—to bounce a basketball off the floor using one hand

goal line—the start of the end zone of a field where a sports team can score

jersey—the shirt of a sports player's uniform

penalty—a punishment for breaking the rules

puck—a hard, round, flat piece of rubber used in ice hockey

referee—someone who supervises a sports match or game and makes sure that the players obey the rules

strike—when all the bowling pins are knocked down with one roll of the ball

Read More

Amoroso, Cynthia, and Robert B. Noyed. *Football.* Jump into Sports. Mankato, Minn.: Child's World, 2009.

Ghigna, Charles. *Score!: 50 Poems to Motivate and Inspire.* New York: Abrams Books for Young Readers, 2008.

Herzog, Brad. *A Is for Amazing Moments: A Sports Alphabet.* Chelsea, Mich.: Sleeping Bear Press, 2008.

Internet Sites

FactHound offers a safe, fun way to find Internet sites related to this book. All of the sites on FactHound have been researched by our staff.

Here's all you do:

Visit www.facthound.com

Type in this code: 9781429652599

Super-cool stuff!

Check out projects, games and lots more at
www.capstonekids.com

Index

A+ Books are published by Capstone Press,
151 Good Counsel Drive, P.O. Box 669, Mankato, Minnesota 56002.
www.capstonepub.com

Copyright © 2011 by Capstone Press, a Capstone imprint.
All rights reserved.
No part of this publication may be reproduced in whole or in part, or stored in a retrieval system,
or transmitted in any form or by any means, electronic, mechanical, photocopying, recording,
or otherwise, without written permission of the publisher.
For information regarding permission, write to Capstone Press,
151 Good Counsel Drive, P.O. Box 669, Dept. R, Mankato, Minnesota 56002.

Books published by Capstone Press are manufactured with paper
containing at least 10 percent post-consumer waste.

Library of Congress Cataloging-in-Publication Data
Salas, Laura Purdie.
  Colors of sports / by Laura Purdie Salas.
    p. cm.—(A+ books. Colors all around)
Includes bibliographical references and index.
Summary: "Simple text and photographs illustrate the colors of sports"—Provided by publisher.
  ISBN 978-1-4296-5259-9 (library binding)
  ISBN 978-1-4296-6149-2 (paperback)
1. Sports—Pictorial works—Juvenile literature. I. Title. II. Series.
GV705.3.S35 2011   2010028412
  796.022'2—dc22

Credits
Jenny Marks, editor; Bobbie Nuytten, designer; Svetlana Zhurkin, media researcher; Eric Manske,
        production specialist

Photo Credits
Alamy/Don Tonge, 14–15
Dreamstime/Lightvision, 10–11
Getty Images/AFP/Yuri Kadobnov, 20–21
iStockphoto/Mark Stahl, 26–27
Photodisc, 1
Shutterstock: background throughout; Andrey Kozachenko, 12–13; bikeriderlondon,
        4–5; Galina Barskaya, 22–23; Maximus Art, 6–7; muzsy, 2–3; Pete Saloutos,
        28–29; Sam Robles, 24–25; Stephen Aaron Rees, 18–19; Tad Denson, 16–17;
        Vaclav Volrab, 8–9; Vitaly Krivosheev, cover

Note to Parents, Teachers, and Librarians
The Colors All Around series supports national arts education standards related to identifying
colors in the environment. This book describes and illustrates colors seen in sports. The images
support early readers in understanding the text. The repetition of words and phrases helps
early readers learn new words. This book also introduces early readers to subject-specific
vocabulary words, which are defined in the Glossary section. Early readers may need
assistance to read some words and to use the Table of Contents, Glossary, Read More,
Internet Sites, and Index sections of the book.

Printed in the United States of America in North Mankato, Minnesota.
092010   005933CGS11